Raspberries fo

Also from the Emma Press:

The Emma Press Anthology of Mildly Erotic Verse
A Poetic Primer for Love and Seduction: Naso was my Tutor
The Emma Press Anthology of Motherhood
The Emma Press Anthology of Fatherhood (May 2014)

The Emma Press Picks:

The Flower and the Plough, by Rachel Piercey
The Emmores, by Richard O'Brien
The Held and the Lost, by Kristen Roberts
Captain Love and the Five Joaquins, by John Clegg (May 2014)

Pamphlets:

Ikhda, by Ikhda, by Ikhda Ayuning Maharsi
The Dead Snail Diaries, by Jamie McGarry (Apr 2014)

Raspberries for the Ferry

by Andrew Wynn Owen

THE EMMA PRESS

For John Fuller

THE EMMA PRESS

First published in Great Britain in 2014
by the Emma Press Ltd

Poems copyright © Andrew Wynn Owen 2014
Introduction copyright © Richard O'Brien 2014

ISBN 978-0-9574596-5-6

A CIP catalogue record of this book
is available from the British Library.

Printed and bound in Great Britain
by Letterworks Ltd, Reading.

theemmapress.com
editor@theemmapress.com

Introduction

Whenever I read a poem by Andrew Wynn Owen, I'm reminded of the song 'Losing My Edge' by LCD Soundsystem: a giddy paean to paranoia from an ageing artist looking nervily over his shoulder at the 'better-looking people with better ideas and more talent', 'the kids' who are 'coming up from behind'. And I'm 23.

At least, that's my first thought. My second is that Andrew's poems skilfully execute a difficult balancing act, between the lightly-borne weight of his literary forebears – John Betjeman, W. H. Auden, Paul Muldoon, Glyn Maxwell, and further back, the rusty glimmer of Anglo-Saxon alliterative verse – and the pure pleasure of their own formal invention.

Which is, of course, what places him in their lineage. He negotiates rhyme, rhythm and structure as nimbly as Houdini negotiated a straitjacket; his ideas are no more boxed in by the shapes which hold them than Escher was limited by the lines of a staircase. At every turn, his language derives a kind of glee from evading its captors, chafing and fretting at its formal constraints until the edges of the lines spit sparks.

Take, for example, 'Raspberries', where thoughts of prelapsarian paradise coax the addressed reader almost imperceptibly into a vision of 'hedon-/istic gymnasts born in Sweden'. The word itself is forced over the line-break into an acrobatic stretch, as if bowing before the divine power of the poem's subject, capable of inspiring admirers both to risk life and to cheat death, and to which 'You' are imagined surrendering in a kind of festive masochism which is the flipside of the poem's decadence.

Part of the pleasure of reading Wynn Owen's work is trying and failing to understand where the twists and turns in his ideas spring from, before simply acceding to their relentless forward motion, like the light in 'Serenade', 'skimming/Sketchily like pen between two points'. Thought is preceded by and discovered in rhythm, a process presented in the last lines of 'Pinwheel' – but where does one end and the other begin? Has life merged into mechanism?

Frequently the poems call attention to their own artificiality; to the kinship they share with the dancer's feet in 'Footage of Nureyev' which at their owner's death are reanimated, unstoppably, as 'the clockwork carousels/the American papers really wanted them to be'.

'Strandbeests', in particular, feels haunted by the idea that the poem itself might be no different to the self-propelling sculptures installed on beaches by the Dutch artist Theo Jansen. These 'biological machines' prompt the speaker to consider his art advancing as if by an elastic power devoid of human agency – 'Am I only tightened string/Spun and tuned to turn a song?' – before ending with a muted endorsement of their uncanny, inhuman progress: 'Let this tame automaton/ Rumble, through its reaches, on.'

And yet elsewhere, this debut pamphlet finds room for real tenderness – sometimes generated by the form itself, as in 'Icarus', where the familiar repetition of a villanelle is used to enwrap rather than entrap, weaving a soft and silky verbal blanket around its fallen subject. Two letter-poems, in the voices of Robert and Elizabeth Barrett Browning, celebrate the way their speakers' love revivifies the world, joy leaping from each line committed to 'this vast expanse of paper where we live'.

Life springs from this scribbling energy, mirrored in the flowing water of 'The Lay of the Lake' and the look in 'Your Smile' which allows the speaker to 'twirl into death carelessly like a leaf'. But Wynn Owen never lets it overwhelm the poems entirely, or mask the very urgency of feeling many of them are constructed to communicate. He says as much himself in 'Serenade', in one of the most revealing moments in a pamphlet whose effervescent personality is visible behind each and every persona: 'I should not write it if it were not true/Or just because I thought it sounded right.'

Richard O'Brien
March 2014

Contents

Raspberries

Available, but not for long,
They look like lesser fruits of Eden.
So sweet they force you into song
And fill your head with dreams of hedon-
istic gymnasts born in Sweden.
These luscious buds should be illegal,
Reserved for emperor and eagle.

Yes, don't they make you salivate?
That danglingness, their regal nods
To passers-by as if to state
A bloodline running back to gods.
You'd like them to arrive in squads
And drag you screaming to a cell
With sticky fists on each lapel.

These friendly triffids catch your eye
Across a busy motorway
And beckon you to have a try.
Their trimming is décolleté
With underbrush for négligée
And crimpled leaves that make you think
Of Cleopatra draped in mink.

The provenance this clustered fruit
Can claim is unlike any berry:
Venusian origins impute
Its power to party and make merry.
When Charon chauffeurs in the ferry
The only bribes to turn his head
Are juicy, globular, and red.

The Phoenix and the Tortoise

Carapace-parapace,
"Phoenix," said Tortoise, "I
Wish I could fly in the
Air as you do.
Life on the ground is so
Damnably difficult –
Rooted and footweary,
Muddy and blue."

Rustlefluff-tusslebluff,
"Tortoise," said Phoenix, "You
Ask for a gift that is
Not mine to give.
You are a plodder and
I am a soarer and
Like-it-or-not, this is
How we must live."

Pusillan-goosillan,
"Nonsense!" said Tortoise, "These
Things can be changed in a
Matter of time.
Don't you recall how I
Outran Achilles who,
Zeno has witnessed, was
Then in his prime?

"Humbledum-pumbledum,
Then there is Aesop, who
Tells in his Fables how
I beat the hare.
So with a record like
Mine it is natural that
I should consider how
Flight might compare."

2

Sniffery-whiffery,
"Twaddle!" said Phoenix, "You'll
Crawl on your belly for
All of your days.
If you'll excuse me, I'm
Due in Arabia,
Guest of the Sultan – he
Welcomes my stays."

Subterfuge-gubterfuge,
"Phoenix," said Tortoise, "I
Fear you are poised for a
Terrible fit –
While we've been talking, I've
Stolen your plumage and
Now I intend to try
Swooping a bit!"

Oddalming-godalming,
Tortoise went gliding while
Phoenix was stripped to the
Tips of his feet.
Let this preposterous
Parable lesson you:
Watch for the Tortoise and
Shelve your conceit.

The Partridge

after the Old English of the Exeter Book

I know of a bird, weird and twitchy
in renown on the wold, the tricksy partridge.
Unlike all those others who brood in woods
to hatch their chicks, she is an eggless, odd
and unbelaying bird. She makes no mother,
glued to eggs: she is the cradle-snatcher,
kidnapper, who nest-jacks. When she broods
it fits like a jacket for a bit. But when she naps
those eggs hatch and the yoke is on her:
fly-away, fledglings, and find your own herd.
This foster-wing, feeder to foreign tongues
is left bereft, short shrift, before they long
for surer service, an unrented parent
and, across forest,
                    hear her croak: it rends
my heart, wreaks havoc with the vocal strings.

Icarus

Gather Calpol, bandage, blanket,
Hot water bottle, wool, and muslin.
Seek for him a floating basket.

Blend the pallor with the palette,
Anoint the head and paint with plantain:
Tend with Calpol, bandage, blanket.

Cross his limbs and tie a garnet
To his temple. Say the Latin
And set for him a floating basket.

Lay him down on silk and velvet.
Wash him in freshwater's fountain.
Treat with Calpol, bandage, blanket.

Listen for life's final ripplet
Breaking at this outer margin:
Line for him a floating basket.

Grieve, resent it, cry in secret
But gather lilac, scatter lupin,
Sprinkle Calpol, bandage, blanket,
And set him in a floating basket.

Footage of Nureyev

The moment he died, Nureyev's feet
turned into the clockwork carousels
the American papers really wanted them to be.
I can hear the shoes whistling in the coffin,
funeral procession getting creeped out –
saying, "This is eerie," up the aisle.
When those calves clicked it was more silent,
dead silent, than the grave, more solemn
than the dance of death or the irate
undertaker's breath. The comrades wept, crept,
then stepped, then leapt, so slick – this
was the miracle, mechanical dance of life.
This was the Stradivarius Humanus in the flesh,
in a gilded wooden crate, clopping away
the ankles into action, then legs, then heart
pulsing forth like a jack-in-the-box, giving
Leningrad the fright of its life. Life in
the pad of this mad, risen Messiah figure,
the living vivre, the synapse triggered yo-yo –
first snowdrop of the cultural thaw was go,
breaking the Two Worlds War. He breathed,
the spinning sylph, on a vesper, divesting death
under the flowers thrown on the stage
for the Lord of the Dance.

                      This was 1960,
the opening night of Don Quixote. Soon
the dancer without defect would defect,
dashing the door off the land of the living.

Charles Bovary's Cap

Shako, sealskin, billycock, and velvet,
this self-incongruous cap was fashioned
for an occasion, which is to say well met
to Bovary's first school, with lozenges
of ornament. Who would be a poet
when he could wear a cap like this, oval
and braced with whalebone, so certainly set
in its ways as a cap, so well shellacked
it seems more collage than cap? I would bet
all the make-believe, fancy-fuss of dress
that this cap, worn but untired, a subset
of grizzly bear and badger, knows something
but what that implies, for the life of it,
I cannot say. So don't get in a flap
about embarrassment, that seismic bait
of breath and wash of shame, because
synapses can rearrange so the upset
was persona-al, never personal –
and yet I feel forced to say this outfit
caterwauls and taunts, cajoles and riddles
me. Its needle-vision is explicit
but too slight: through this or that interstice
what would attack the retina – a spit
of arsenic, a blench of unbecoming,
or unblinking bloodshot eye, a blanket?
It makes me think of parachutes falling
opulently overhead, the close-knit
stitchedness of time unravelling now,
divulging its weft and longestkept secret.

Serenade

The lights wink out on most of London now.
Stubborn beacons blare from office blocks
And will keep blaring till the sun shows up
Apologetically tomorrow with
Armfuls of mango, tanqueray, concern
And ancientworldy stories about goats.

Am I a fan of light? I think I am.
I should not write it if it were not true
Or just because I thought it sounded right.
I like the way light is not really here
Or there but constantly in motion, skimming
Sketchily like pen between two points.
I tried to trap light in a calvacade
Of swinging mirrors but the tinted glass
Insists on snatching or refracting bits.
Reflective – but that only goes so far.

Am I in love with light? I guess I am.
Kaleidoscopic autumn flicking off
Solicitations from a folding world;
A winter missionary, redeeming weight
From thinnest, indistinguishable things;
The hoop it chucks festooningly in spring
To tangle grieving in its greenish limbs;
Or, in the summer, judders over trees
In hot indulgence of the gasping leaves.
Verbs I know for light are basking words.

The lights switch off on most of London now
And as they flick, the buildings seem to bow.
Night sets a new complexion on the city
Where all my thoughts, my lantern, turn on you.
I promise, like the sun will rise tomorrow,
I would not write this if it were not true.

The Lay of the Lake

The mist on the lake is like smoke from your lips.
It glides and it floats, then it flutters and flips.
It flirts with the air and it simmers and churns,
It splashes and pashes and runs and returns,
It rises in columns, it covers the sand,
It alters my pulse like your hand in my hand.

The lake is lagooning, tomfooling and crooning,
It oboes and flutes and it honks with basooning,
It switches and snatches and waxes dramatic,
It glugs and it gulps and it schmoozes aquatic,
It japes at the rocks and it judders retreat
And jostles the swash as it laps at my feet.

The lake is a behemoth hacking a lair,
The lake is a creature with flyaway hair,
The lake is Charybdis convening the spray,
The lake is the ghoul in a miracle play,
The lake is where fisherman Andrew was called
To cast off his line, where he travelled and trawled.

The water is skirting and scuffing my feet,
The water is clicking and sharing a tweet,
The water is ribbons and cashmere and mess,
The water's a starlet unstrapping her dress,
The water's your voice, like a stone in my shoe,
The water's the flow and the substance of you.

The lake will be silent and sullen and still.
And the water will freeze, as in winter it will.
The trees will be fossil and silted in oil,
The solarflare wind will unseason the soil,
And the mist will no longer resemble the smoke
You blew in a ring round my tongue for a joke.

Robert Browning in Piazza San Felice

The love that moves the sun and other stars
moves me today, Elizabeth, to write
to you, from the via by our casa's

rusticated front while in the sunlight
kids play on the Palazzo Pitti's plunge
of cobblestoning hill. The deft termite

of history has seen the city lunge
far out here, fashioned out of Tuscany
and bookkeeping, while overhead the sponge

of heaven absorbs everything we see
in capillaries of line and iamb
which we will hear hereafter – I précis

this shaky simile because I am
so happy, life-hallowed, the carp that swim
in the Arno know, the leaves by the dam

rustle knowledge of it, and the pilgrim
stops short to wish me well (you have unshut
the sunadmitting door of that poem

I adumbrate with each syllable!) but
there is a vital image I have missed:
in Milan a bark of steam coconuts

the accidental air as the calm abbess
steps lightly from her carriage out at Monza
and finds it necessary to confess

to anyone who'll listen that the summa
theologica of her girlhood was
engine travel. Later, at her escritoire,

she'll gush of that which had begun its course
when, swooping far out from Fiesole's
fold, Leonardo gave to Daedalus's

story better wings. The churn of industry's
lung found pneuma and more to spare. What is left
are those young voices moving through galleries

like wind through the ladybird's empty craft
which, hollowed by the summer, waits for winter
when the snows and showers will set it adrift.

Elizabeth Barrett Browning outside Casa Guidi

Emerging from our home to see the stars
I read your letter and reflect on it;
this city that we live in is not ours

though you (for all your puppetries of wit)
would kill to call yourself a Florentine.
You'd be 'Roberto de Medici' (lit

with hanging lanterns, allocating wine
by bucketload to clients who lift your car
above the Arno's course, an endless line

processing past the Ponte Trinita
to kneel before your rustic frontispiece
emblazoned with the Citrus Medica).

Yes, you would be Lorenzo – I, Clarice!
I cannot say it charms. (You claim you want
to predecease me and, en route to peace,

bestrew my way with fleur-de-lis. What cant
you talk, what terms you couch it in!) Forgive
the world and smile. Each page is our enceinte –

this vast expanse of paper where we live
was given as a palace for our selves
(and alter egos). No alternative

excels it as a dwelling: here are shelves
containing other worlds beyond our reach
that pen and ink can penetrate, where delves

of brambledens and foxgloves govern speech
(and in their speaking, take an agnomen
as symbol of their office). We must teach

the gap between the heron and the wren
to see reflourishings. (The hanging head
of Atlas will be raised upright again

when Hesperis rebeckons him to bed.)
You know your way so saddle up: though heat
may scatter, love will not divide (instead,

you groan of sweetly sad (and sadly sweet!)) –
when love inspects the field and speaks her mind,
a ripple spreads through the (like water) wheat.

The Trees

Autumn enters and we, hats off, salute
new winds. Hello, howler! Goodbye, leaf-lives!
Your flourish was so late this year, so late.

We will have many stories to relate
about the rustling, buffeting, the blithe
entrance of Autumn which we, hats off, salute.

Your closeness is the reason we elate
and throwing greenness to the wind, we thrive
on a voice that is so late, this year so late.

Nothing now can temper or dilute
the happiness we have. We'll pay our tithe
when Autumn enters and we, hats off, salute.

There's nothing we've longed longer to translate
than your all-forgiving hush, that lithe
and vibrant voice, so late this year, so late.

We've served our sentence being separate
and now it's time to party: Winter's wife,
Autumn enters and we, hats off, salute
your voice that is (so late this year) so late.

Walk

So I need a rhythm, a beat, a fold
in vibrations flowing through the feet –
call it repetition, old condition, but either way
I need to make the floor want more. Force
the face of the earth to pathfind for me. Scrunch
the toes, wiggle them, squiggle the mud, bend
arches like Philoctetes bow. You know
they're made for you to screw up. Scrapes
you get into now are practice. The world
is a forest and a forest, if you see it for
the trees, is a field. Filed under 'f'. Foot:
appendage – one letter pen of steps. No prob.
Energy and entropy are next – they net
together, do their duet, make ripples. Leave
a line to think on that. It's important later.

OK. Carry on. Keep the air pumping,
the organic winches and levers in the legs working
like a band of tubas, in concert. Orchestrate
it all, same time signature behind you but don't
swivel, nozzle or look back. Let everything flow
and nuzzle up. Clear the atmosphere. Mismanaged
mist can scupper us. Don't kick. Oil
the food pipes, fuel the pneumatic
chambers. Dancing is next week.

Place one foot
                    in front of the other.
Simple.

Insomnia Song

I slept with a terrible crick in my neck.
It buckled my bones and it nobbled my back.
It took me an hour to unclick and relax
And left me convinced that my spine was convex.
I've crashed in a carpark, reposed in a skip
I've dozed in a ditch and I've kipped on a slope
But guilt was the hardest to sleep on of all.
It prickles like hawthorn, it rankles like hell.

I slept with my conscience inverted and splayed.
It prickled my elbow and needled my side.
I tried to roll over. It trampled my head.
I hollered for mercy but it took no heed.
I've snored on a pavement, I've snoozed out on roads
Been drowsy on haystacks and rested on reeds
But never again will I speak as I did
Since guilt cantered in and decamped in my head.

I slept like a rock on a tectonic fault.
My fingernails scratched and I scrunched up my feet.
It felt like the army was out on parade
And using my spine as a substitute road.
I've caught forty winks on the back of a yak
And copped a few Z's at the wheel of a truck
But, darling, that's nothing to how I was pained
When guilt called me in for a piece of his mind.

I slept with a pain that I couldn't pin down;
It dug at my body from dusk until dawn.
I tried to use reason to winkle it out
But all my surmises transpired to be moot.
I've drowsed on the decking where flatfishes slap
And sleeping on foot was one hell of a schlep
But guilt is an earwig that burrows inside
And triggers the neurons where nightmares are made.

I slept like a man who has spoken offhand
To one on whose life all his prospects are pinned.
It's stupid to argue – I know I was wrong –
So here are some words you can wear like a ring:
I've nodded in armchairs, I've catnapped in crates
I've flopped on chaise longues and I've languished on roots
But nothing prepared me for how I would ache
When guilt got my number and came for the week.

I slept with a tortuous twist in my hips.
It jittered like caffeine and scrambled my hopes
Of blinking away with the blankness of rest,
Corrupting my senses, kyboshing my drift.
I slumbered in barrels and zonked out on kegs,
Siestaed with scarecrows and bunked up with pigs
But guilt laid a bed that put paid to the lot
And raddled my brain as it riddled my heart.

I slept like a mouse in a nest full of snakes;
Guilt prickled my hackles and got in my nooks.
I wriggled and writhed but it wrapped me in coils,
Constricting my lungs and constraining my heels.
I've slouched in a fountain, I've slumped on a bench,
I've conked in a station and lolled in a bunch
Of poisonous places I quail to recall
But guilt is the hardest, it rankles like hell.

Of all of the poisons that bring about death,
The stew mixed by guilt is the nastiest broth.
Yes, aconite bites and can make you convulse
And mercury kicks and will weaken your pulse
And strychnine is yucky and crumples the lungs
And hemlock's the worst and will lick you with pangs
But hemlock is pop next to guilt's bedtime cup.
Life's toxic like this! Can we kiss and make up?

I'm sorry I said what I did and repent.
Yes, since you departed, I can't see the point
In waking or walking or talking or play
So this is a song I have turned to a plea:
Once 'love' was a word I was lost to pronounce
But now that I've practised, I'm taking my chance –
Let's throw in together and gather our wits
To expiate guilt and ungenerous thoughts!

I slept with a bonecracking crick in my neck
But longed all the while for your breath on my back
So settle with me and let's call it a day –
We shan't be cut short and we shall not be coy.
Delight is the god I'm delighted to serve
And you are the prophet he sent me to love
So let's cast away care and be free as we like
And guilt will ride off on his rickety bike.

Strandbeests

"I want to put these forms of life on the beaches and they should survive there in the future, learning to live on their own" – Theo Jansen

From the land of windmills, look!
Rolling over rock and fleck,
Gadgets gallop up the sand,
Tilting with a ticking sound.
While the beasts of stick and sail
Scramble over slate and shale,
Biological machines
Interweave their clowning scenes.

Stickmen, Lowry said, are what
Bodies are beneath their wit,
Stretched in smiles across a face
Pulled to fluster or confess.
Am I only tightened string
Spun and tuned to turn a song?
Vectored in my groove, I can't
Shift an inch. I sit and chant.

Think, aficionado, if
Clock and map enclose a life,
What reconnaissance is new?
Binaries of yes and no
Are the grub of ogres, gods,
Sherpas, Lonely Planet guides –
Turf I cannot wish my own,
Free to doodle, yarn and yawn.

Water, once the walker's wall,
Washes clothes and churns the wheel –
Water, where the simplest cells
Clustered out of molecules.
Like the water, let this stick
Find a spot to fix a stake.
Let this tame automaton
Rumble, through its reaches, on.

The Whale

after the Old English of the Exeter Book

I sing of a fish, with all my wiles
in woven words, of the wondrous whale.
He often appears to unwary wanderers
fierce and unfriendly to all seafarers,
to many a man. He is called Fastitocalon,
this flubber of the ocean lanes.
He resembles a rock roughly eroded
or a seething straggle of strangleweed
bounded by sandbanks, basking offshore
so seafarers think they have spotted shelter.

Now they fix their high-keeled ship
to this trick-land with unravelled rope
and tether the sea-steeds at ocean's edge;
they climb to the top of that ridge
in strong spirits; their ships saunter
sturdy by shore, surrounded by water.
At length the tired crew pitch tents,
bearing no further fears of disturbance.
There, on the summit, a fire is fuelled
and a blaze built; they are all heartened
but bent-double, they rankle for rest.
When the master monster, the briny beast,
supposes the sailors are sound asleep
and kip in camp, content with the weather,
he suddenly slides under the surface;
he speedily dives to his shadowy bed,
delivering sailors and ships to drown
in the Doors of Death.
                              That's also the deal with demons,
the Faustpact-forgers who, by lying,
lure our best men with mischievous magicking;
they guile them from God with sordid sorcery

and lead them a dance so they tragically try
for a monster's clemency and, at the close,
are dragged down by that friend-foe.
When the devious demon is certain
the Sons of Man, after terrible torture,
are totally brainwashed, bound to his will,
with cunning intelligence he becomes their killer –
sinners who spread his evil on earth,
overreaching and ruthless. Now, under cover
of his enchanted helmet, he digs down to Hell,
that system of circles, that endless abyss
below the mists, just as the whale
scuppers seafarers, both sailors and ships.

But mighty whale, the water-traveller,
knows another miracle still more marvellous.
If he is hungry when wandering
and the beast's belly moans for feasting,
the ocean-warden widens his mouth,
moving his lips. A sweet scent glides out
and gallons of fish are gulled inside,
thrashing towards the source of the smell
and thronging together, a heedless heap
that jam-packs his jaw. So, in a swipe,
those unprisable chops imprison their prey.

Terragogous

Rock-reptilian, land bound, looking round,
cumbersome thundersome, the wondersome survivor.

Schildkröten, ground besotten, age rotten,
wide thrown, seed sown, unknown.

Abdominally-all, steady canopic crawl,
Terragogous, analogous, one solus.

Rising up, mountain top, tired not,
mountaineer, buccaneer, aged seer.

Strong, striking pillar, salad killer,
Desert tracker, can't walk back-er.

Tortue, fought-few, end due, never new,
Stronghold, bulky bold, winter-told.

Armoured for battle, a pebble rattle, tiny cattle,
Mud spattered, shell flattered, egg shattered.

Tartaruga, shambling mover, ancient hoover,
blithering, dithering, all withering.

Lizard face, mammoth base, body-mace,
Lion claws, bear-scaled paws, plated sores.

Testudo, Greek named, truculent-famed,
Unmatched, unmastered, untamed, unreal.

Steadfast thing, resilient king,
Shuffling, ruffling, tussling boulder.

Ancestry great, dino-fate, Jurassic-late,
Wizened race, egg based, carapaced.

Your Smile

It arrests me today, happiness spun in skin –
landscape sculpted from life's lightest discursiveness
and a scene that I, breath-batedly, wait to scan.
I'm a fool for your tongue, neck for your laughter's noose,
and I'd sing, if I could, tributes in Ancient Norse.
Love, I think you're the grain ground in my labours' mill.
I could wither and wilt, waiting for you to smile.

It's the law of my eye always to seek out charm
and I'd follow your smile far as my feet can run.
I could live on your lips, calling their corners home,
and enshrine all the words, slowly in rhyme and rune,
that you spill like the split-seconding sound of rain.
It's a marvel to me world has a you within,
where the ripples you make meet me at every turn.

When that time is at hand, time to relinquish life,
I'll remember your smile breaking and burning on
and I'll twirl into death carelessly like a leaf
that has spread in the fresh force of the Tuscan sun.
Yes, you're all of the thrill, none of the fall, of sin
and the heat that I feel, looking you eye-to-lip,
is the proof of two selves starting to overlap.

Pinwheel

Pinwheel, spinner of sails, speeder of time, you go
roundabout with a fin-twirl, with a circle-curl
and a tick of the wind. Toysomely be and, gee!
go with fullness of grace, toil with the wind's reveal
to revolve as you stand, pivot and reel and trail
air in shapely entwines. Blaze and amazement-make!
Be my clattering lynchpin and my workman's mark.

Hypnotiser of gadflies and this gadabout
(that's me, lolling around reading by riversides),
clap the pulse of the seaboard and the sandy beat.
Weathervane, you are wind-wonder, composed of shards,
and your paperiness stills as the storm recedes.
That abandoner, love, cannot eclipse your play,
stick-stuck automobile powered by a simple ploy.

Turbo-trinket, record carefully air's assent
to the marriage of page-tech and the climate's test:
time is flourisher, gear-change, and your patron saint
while you, miniature windmill, your effusive twist
is the sign of my plan, saving this craft from waste.
You're a rhythm refreshed, quickened, and with this piece
I feel thoughts I mislaid slowly are finding place.

Acknowledgments

'Strandbeests' refers to the kinetic sculptures of Theo Jansen.

'The Partridge' and 'The Whale' are free translations from the Old English of *The Exeter Book*.

'Pinwheel' and 'Your Smile' are written in accentual asclepiads, prompted by W. H. Auden's 'In Due Season'.

I would like to thank all the members of The Florio Society at Magdalen College, Oxford, where many of these poems were first presented.

I would also like to give special thanks to John Fuller, Peter Carpenter, Doriel Hulse, Archie Cornish, Will Humphries, Lorna Oakley, Gabriel Rolfe, Frank Lawton, John Phipps, Richard O'Brien, Emma Wright, Martin Amis, and Tom Wynn Owen.

About the poet

Andrew Wynn Owen is reading for a BA in English Language and Literature at Magdalen College, Oxford. He is a former winner of the Foyle Young Poets of the Year Award, the Ledbury Poetry Competition, The Times Stephen Spender Prize for poetry translation, and The Richard Selig Prize. He is currently Secretary of the Oxford University Poetry Society and co-editor of The Mays anthology for 2014.

The Emma Press

small press, big dreams

The Emma Press is an independent publisher dedicated to
producing books which are sweet, funny and beautiful.
It was founded in 2012 in Winnersh, UK, by Emma Wright
and the first Emma Press book, *The Flower and the Plough* by
Rachel Piercey, was published in January 2013.

Our current publishing programme includes a mixture of
themed poetry anthologies and single-author pamphlets, with
an ongoing engagement with the works of the Roman poet Ovid.
We publish poems and books which excite us, and we are
often on the lookout for new writing.

Visit our website and sign up to the Emma Press newsletter
to hear about all upcoming calls for submissions as well as our
events and publications. You can also purchase our other titles
and poetry-related stationery in our online shop.

http://theemmapress.com

Also from the Emma Press:

THE EMMA PRESS ANTHOLOGY MOTHERHOOD
ISBN: 978 0 9574596 7 0 / PRICE: £10

Love and devotion sit alongside exhaustion and doubt in this profoundly moving collection of poems about mothers and the state of motherhood, with poems from Kathryn Maris, Catherine Smith, Ikhda Ayuning Maharsi and Clare Pollard.

IKHDA, BY IKHDA
BY: Ikhda Ayuning Maharsi / ISBN: 978 0 9574596 6 3 / PRICE: £6.50

Characters and landscapes leap off every page in Ikhda Ayuning Maharsi's dazzling first pamphlet. The poems pulse with a visceral femininity and humanity as Maharsi glories in the possibilities of language and life.

THE HELD AND THE LOST
BY: Kristen Roberts / ISBN: 978 0 9574596 8 7 / PRICE: £5

Emerging Australian poet Kristen Roberts sketches sympathetic portraits of characters and relationships against the backdrop of swaying eucalypts, roses and occasional rain. These are love poems with their eyes open and scars defiantly on display.

THE EMMORES
BY: Richard O'Brien / ISBN: 978 0 9574596 4 9 / PRICE: £5

Richard O'Brien deploys every trick in the love poet's book in this fascinating pamphlet, written in response to a new long-distance relationship. An irresistible mix of tender odes, introspective sonnets, exuberant free verse and anthems of sexual persuasion.